Ten of the Best: Stories of Exploration and Adventure

TEN OF THE BEST ADVENTURES IN
THE SKY

Crabtree Publishing Company
www.crabtreebooks.com

Crabtree Publishing Company
www.crabtreebooks.com
1-800-387-7650

Publishing in Canada
616 Welland Ave.
St. Catharines, ON
L2M 5V6

Published in the United States
PMB 59051, 350 Fifth Ave.
59th Floor,
New York, NY

Published in **2016 by CRABTREE PUBLISHING COMPANY.**

Printed in Canada/082015/BF20150630

Project development, design, and concept:
  David West Children's Books

Author and designer: David West

Illustrator: David West

Contributing editor: Steve Parker

Editor: Kathy Middleton

Proofreader: Kelly Spence

**Production coordinator
  and Prepress technician**: Ken Wright

Print coordinator: Margaret Amy Salter

Library and Archives Canada Cataloguing in Publication

West, David, 1956-, author
    Ten of the best adventures in the sky / David West.

(Ten of the best : stories of exploration and adventure)
Includes index.
Issued in print and electronic formats.
ISBN 978-0-7787-1838-3 (bound).--
ISBN 978-0-7787-1873-4 (paperback).--
ISBN 978-1-4271-7806-0 (pdf).--ISBN 978-1-4271-7800-8 (html)

    1. Flight--History--Juvenile literature. 2. Aeronautics--History--
Juvenile literature. 3. Air pilots--Juvenile literature. I. Title. II. Title:
Adventures in the sky.

TL515.W47 2015   j629.1309   C2015-903040-4
                                            C2015-903041-2

Library of Congress Cataloging-in-Publication Data

West, David, 1956- author.
 Ten of the best adventures in the sky / David West.
    pages cm. -- (Ten of the best: stories of exploration and
adventure)
 Includes index.
 ISBN 978-0-7787-1838-3 (reinforced library binding : alk. paper) --
ISBN 978-0-7787-1873-4 (pbk. : alk. paper) --
ISBN 978-1-4271-7806-0 (electronic pdf : alk. paper) --
ISBN 978-1-4271-7800-8 (electronic html : alk. paper)
 1. Aeronautics--History--Juvenile literature. 2. Air pilots--History-
-Juvenile literature. I. Title.

TL547.W445 2016
629.1309--dc23
                                    2015014851

CONTENTS

First to Fly

François Laurent,
Marquis d'Arlandes

On September 19, 1783, the first living things to float in a basket attached to a balloon lifted off in front of King Louis XVI and Queen Marie Antoinette of France at the royal palace in Versailles. The craft landed safely after an eight-minute flight that covered 1.9 miles (3 km). The passengers were a sheep, a duck, and a rooster.

The balloon was the invention of the Montgolfier brothers in partnership with successful wallpaper manufacturer Jean-Baptiste Réveillon. The balloon's **envelope** was made of silky taffeta cloth coated with **alum** to make it fireproof. Beneath the envelope, a heater burned wool, straw, and old shoes, creating a rich, heavy smoke. The brothers believed, wrongly, that the thick smoke was a gas that was lighter than air that made the balloon rise.

Soon after their successful flight with the balloon full of animals, Étienne Montgolfier and Réveillon started work on a bigger balloon that could carry people. It was about 75 feet (22.9 m) tall and about 50 feet (15.2 m) in diameter. By October 15, 1783, the balloon was ready. Étienne was the first to go up, with the balloon tethered to the ground. Later that day, a science teacher named Pilâtre de Rozier became the second person to rise to an **altitude** of 80 feet (24 m).

On November 21, 1783, Pilâtre and an army officer, the Marquis d'Arlandes, took off from the Château de la Muette on the outskirts of Paris, in the presence of the king. They flew to a height of 3,000 feet (914 m) for a distance of 5.6 miles (9 km). After 25 minutes, they descended and landed among the windmills on the Butte-aux-Cailles, outside the city walls of Paris.

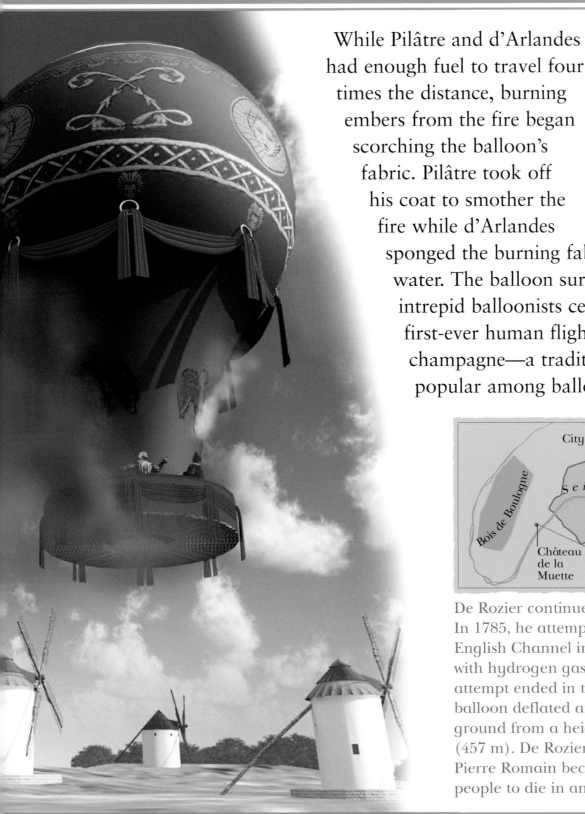

While Pilâtre and d'Arlandes had enough fuel to travel four times the distance, burning embers from the fire began scorching the balloon's fabric. Pilâtre took off his coat to smother the fire while d'Arlandes sponged the burning fabric with water. The balloon survived and the intrepid balloonists celebrated the first-ever human flight by drinking champagne—a tradition that is still popular among balloonists today.

Jean-François Pilâtre de Rozier

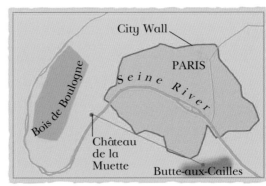

De Rozier continued ballooning. In 1785, he attempted to cross the English Channel in a balloon fueled with hydrogen gas and hot air. The attempt ended in tragic failure. The balloon deflated and crashed to the ground from a height of 1,500 feet (457 m). De Rozier and his friend Pierre Romain became the first people to die in an air crash.

Rooftop Escape

Alberto Santos-Dumont

Alberto Santos-Dumont was an aviation pioneer who lived in Paris, France. Originally from Brazil, he was the heir of a wealthy family of coffee producers. Santos-Dumont designed, built, and flew the first steerable balloon, called a dirigible. He showed the world that controlled flight was possible. Unlike hot air balloons, these airships were filled with hydrogen—a gas lighter than air. Santos-Dumont was wealthy, owning an airship shed and a building for making hydrogen at France's Aéro-Club flying grounds in the Parc Saint Cloud.

In 1900, wealthy French businessman Henri Deutsch de la Meurthe offered a prize of 100,000 francs to the first person who was able to fly a machine from the Parc Saint Cloud to the Eiffel Tower in Paris and back—in under thirty minutes. Santos-Dumont was determined to win and set about building his dirigible.

On August 8, 1901, Santos-Dumont was spotted flying his dirigible above the rooftops of Paris in an attempt to win the prize. Suddenly, the dirigible began to lose its shape as gas leaked from the envelope. It started to lose height and crashed into the side of the Trocadero Hotel. Santos-Dumont was left hanging precariously in his basket as people below stared up in horror. With the help of the fire **brigade**, Santos-Dumont managed to safely climb onto the roof of the hotel. The aviator was unharmed, but his dirigible was ruined.

Just over a month later on October 19, Santos-Dumont succeeded in his quest and claimed the Deutsch prize. He became a celebrity in Europe and throughout the world. Often seen floating above the rooftops in his smaller No. 9 Baladeuse dirigible, he would sometimes land at a fashionable cafe for lunch. Santos-Dumont went on to experiment with heavier-than-air aircraft. He became the first person to fly one in Europe and designed and built the Demoiselle, a **monoplane** with a top speed of over 62 mph (100 kph).

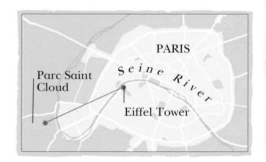

PARIS

Parc Saint Cloud

Seine River

Eiffel Tower

Fatal Plane Crash

Wilbur and Orville Wright

On December 17, 1903, the Wright brothers each made two flights in their Wright Flyer I at Kill Devil Hills near Kitty Hawk, North Carolina. Orville made history inventing the first controlled, powered flight of a heavier-than-air flying machine. He had flown 120 feet (37 m) in 12 seconds, at 6.8 miles per hour (10.9 kph). During the last flight, Wilbur traveled 200 feet (61 m), but damaged the plane on landing.

Over the next few years, the brothers developed their flying machine into the first **fixed-wing** aircraft. It was the brothers' intention to get orders from around the world to build airplanes. Wilbur went to France and performed public demonstrations of their Flyer on August 8, 1908. Stunned onlookers watched as he flew in a circle, making effortless turns. In September, Orville was successfully demonstrating a similar Flyer to the United States army in Virginia. In both cases, the planes had been modified so they could carry a second person.

To get the U.S. army contract, Orville had to prove that the airplane could carry passengers successfully. The first two trials went well—but the third was a disaster. Twenty-six-year-old Lieutenant Thomas E. Selfridge was chosen to be the passenger in the third test. On September 17, Selfridge sat next to Orville as he flew three laps over the parade ground at an altitude of approximately 150 feet (45.7 m). Suddenly, Orville heard a light tapping sound behind him. Looking around, he could see nothing wrong. But before he could shut off the engine and glide to the ground, he heard two large bangs which shook the machine.

A propeller had broken on the Flyer. The plane suddenly veered to the right. As Orville tried to correct the movement, the aircraft nosedived toward the ground. The crowd of spectators cried out as they watched the plane hit the ground with a sickening crunch.

Army troops hurried toward the crash site to recover Orville and Selfridge. The pilot and his passenger were dragged from the wreckage and given first aid as they waited in pain for the ambulance to arrive.

Fort Myer

USA

Kitty Hawk

ATLANTIC OCEAN

After the crash, Orville was still conscious and had suffered some broken ribs and a broken leg. He made a complete recovery. Lieutenant Selfridge was not so lucky—he died shortly afterward from a fractured skull. He was the first person to die in a powered airplane crash.

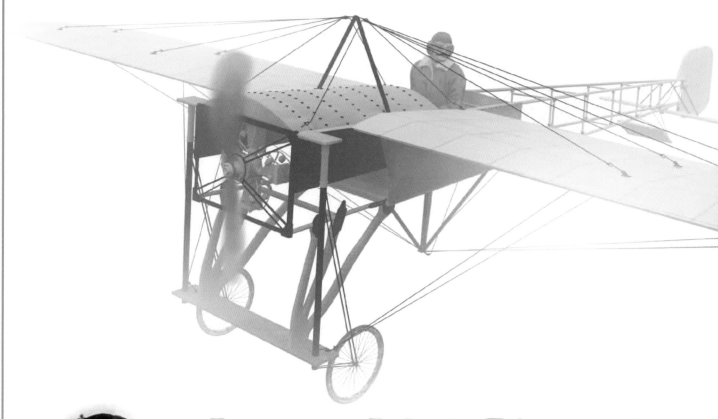

Lost in Mid-Channel

Louis Blériot

In 1909 the *Daily Mail* newspaper in England offered a £1,000 prize for a successful crossing of the English Channel in a heavier-than-air aircraft. British pilot Hubert Latham, the firm favorite to win the prize, took off from Cap Blanc-Nez, near Sangatte, France, on July 19, 1909. After only 8 miles (13 km), his Antoinette IV suffered engine failure and Latham had to **ditch** in the Channel. He was rescued by a French **destroyer**. Back in France, he heard the news that French aviator Louis Blériot had entered the competition.

On Wednesday, July 21, Blériot arrived in France and set up camp near Calais. It was very windy—unsuitable weather for flying. On July 22, Latham's replacement airplane arrived, and he was ready to try again. The wind on the following two days was still too strong, but by Saturday evening

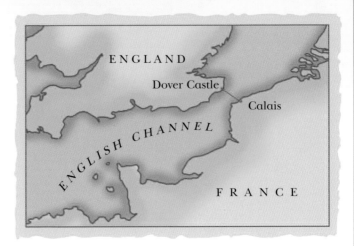

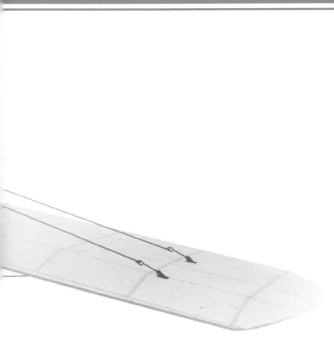

it began to drop, raising hopes in both camps. On July 25, Blériot took off shortly after sunrise. Despite the early hour, an excited crowd gathered to watch. He did not take a compass since he would be following a destroyer.

Flying at approximately 45 mph (72 kph) and at an altitude of about 250 feet (76 m), Blériot soon overtook the ship. Not long afterward, visibility worsened and he was utterly lost, with no visual clues to show him which way to fly. Without a compass, he couldn't double-check to see if he was even heading in the right direction. Blériot was worried, but the weather conditions cleared after a little more than ten minutes. With relief, he recognized the white cliffs of the English coast.

The wind had increased, and Blériot discovered that he had been blown off course. Flying level with the coast, he soon spotted Charles Fontaine, a French newspaper correspondent, waving France's flag to signal him. Heading inland, Blériot landed at Northfall Meadow, close to Dover Castle.

The flight had taken 36 minutes and 30 seconds. Blériot had won the coveted prize. Latham's team hadn't noticed the change in conditions early enough. By the time they were ready to take off, the weather had changed again and it was too windy to fly.

Across the Atlantic

Arthur Whitten Brown and John Alcock

In 1913, the *Daily Mail* newspaper again offered £10,000, this time to whomever could cross the Atlantic Ocean nonstop by airplane. British Royal Navy pilot John Alcock, who had flown in World War I, volunteered to pilot a bomber for British airplane manufacturer Vickers.

Swayed by Alcock's enthusiasm, Vickers agreed. Alcock's navigator was another ex-serviceman, Arthur Brown, who studied aerial **navigation** while he was a prisoner of war.

In May of 1919, Alcock and Brown traveled with their Vimy bomber to the starting point in Newfoundland, Canada, hoping no one else had already accomplished the feat. Their rivals were ready, but luck was on the British duo's side. On May 18, the Martinsyde team's plane was wrecked taking off from rough ground. The Sopwith team got airborne, only to ditch in the sea 24 hours later with an overheated engine. The Handley Page team were grounded, waiting for a replacement for a clogged radiator. Alcock and Brown carefully scouted for a flat takeoff field. Alcock suspected that the island's water might be causing all the engine problems, so before the flight he had their radiator water filtered three times to remove any heavy minerals.

On June 14, they took off in a howling storm. They intended to navigate using the newly invented **radio compass**, but the wind had damaged it, making it useless. Alcock took them as high as he could to try and navigate by the stars. But it was so cold up there that ice began to build up on the

instruments. Brown unbuckled himself to chip away at it. The controls became heavier. Alcock looked around and saw in horror ice building up on the plane's wings. He signaled to Brown to go out. Brown inched along the wing hacking at the ice, but it was slow work. Alcock signaled Brown to hold on tight, then dove down toward the ocean. At 50 feet (15 m) they broke through the clouds. The tops of the wave were visible. Alcock fought the controls and they leveled out, barely clearing the water. But it had worked—the ice was gone!

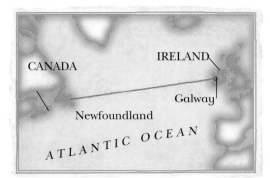

CANADA
IRELAND
Galway
Newfoundland
ATLANTIC OCEAN

After 16 hours, they finally reached Galway, in Ireland. They spotted a field to land in, but onlookers tried to wave them on. It was a **bog**! Before the flight, Alcock had removed the nose wheel to reduce **drag**. As they touched down, the plane pitched forward and crumpled into the soft soil—both pilots emerged unharmed to be hailed as heroes.

Solo Across the Atlantic

The Orteig Prize offered $25,000 for the first successful nonstop flight made between New York City and Paris. The prize attracted a group of well known, highly experienced, and well-financed pilots. There was one exception, a 25-year-old unknown named Charles Lindbergh, who was an American airmail pilot. He had a $15,000 bank loan, a $1,000 donation, and $2,000 of his own savings. A newly designed monoplane was to be built by the Ryan Aircraft Company. Named the *Spirit of St. Louis*, the fabric-covered monoplane was designed by the Ryan Company's chief engineer and Lindbergh.

Charles Lindbergh

Six aviators had already died trying to win the Orteig Prize before Lindbergh took off from Roosevelt Field on May 20, 1927. Lindbergh had made every effort to cut down on weight in the plane, even cutting the top and bottom off his flight map. The plane, carrying 2,710 pounds (1,230 kg) of fuel, just managed to clear the telephone lines at the far end of the field as it climbed into the sky.

Lindbergh sat in a cramped cockpit on a stiff wicker seat. He had to look out of the side windows to see ahead since the plane had no front windows. Fighting ice buildup, flying blind through fog for hours, navigating by the stars, and suffering a mounting need for sleep all pushed Lindbergh's endurance to the limit. At one point, Lindbergh skimmed storm clouds at 10,000 feet (3,000 m). To stay awake, he removed *Spirit's* window and descended close enough to the ocean for spray off the waves to revive him. After 25 hours, Lindbergh spotted a fishing boat. Leaning out of the window he yelled, "Which way is Ireland?"

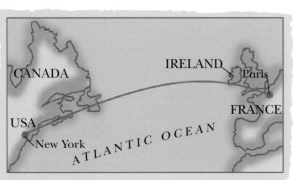

After 38 hours, at 10:22 pm, Lindbergh reached Le Bourget Airport outside Paris. A large crowd had gathered, and he had to take extra care to miss them as he landed. Excited people dragged him out of the cockpit and paraded him on their shoulders for half an hour before police could rescue him.

Southern Cross

A Fokker trimotor monoplane, named the Southern Cross, was flown by Australian aviator Charles Kingsford Smith and his crew from the United States to Australia, a distance of about 7,250 miles (11,670 km).

Charles Kingsford Smith

Kingsford Smith and his copilot Charles Ulm took off on the first leg of their journey in the *Southern Cross* from Oakland, California, on May 31, 1928. The flight was uneventful and lasted 27 hours and 25 minutes. In Hawaii, they refueled and took off again, headed for Suva, Fiji.

Far from land, one of the engines suddenly started coughing and sputtering. This continued for eight anxious minutes, and the men were relieved when it stopped. Their constant worry, however, was running out of gasoline. Frequent storms meant they had to climb high above the clouds, using up valuable fuel. The storms were severe, but the 3,155-mile (5,077 km) flight was safely completed in just over 34 hours. At that time, it was the longest-ever flight across an ocean. As the crew stepped off the plane, they were greeted by happy Fijians. But they discovered the constant roar of the engines had made them temporarily deaf.

The final flight from Fiji to Brisbane was the shortest of the three legs, but it proved to be the worst leg of the entire crossing. Tropical rainstorms lashed the plane, and water seeped through the windshield, drenching Kingsford Smith and Ulm. They were continually thrown around the cabin as the storms rocked the plane. Neither pilot was buckled in. At one point they had to climb to 9,022 feet (2,750 m) to avoid a storm. The plane had no

control over air pressure and no heater—the crew almost froze. At times the storm made the plane suddenly drop by more than 300 feet (91.5 m). Both Kingsford Smith and Ulm had to man the controls to keep the plane from diving into the ocean. They finally landed safely in Australia at Ballina, south of Brisbane— 20 hours after takeoff.

A crowd of 15,000 fans gathered at Ballina airport on June 9, 1928. Kingsford Smith and his crew had achieved the first trans-Pacific flight. On November 8, 1935, while attempting to break the England to Australia record, Kingsford Smith and Ulm disappeared in the Andaman Sea off Burma.

Lost in the Pacific

After setting many solo flight records, including becoming the first woman to fly solo nonstop across the Atlantic Ocean, American pilot Amelia Earhart decided to plan an around-the-world flight. Her first attempt failed when her Lockheed Electra was damaged during takeoff.

Amelia Earhart

On May 20, 1937, Earhart took off from Oakland, California with Fred Noonan as her navigator. After stops in South America, Africa, India, and Southeast Asia, the Lockheed Electra arrived at Lae, New Guinea, on June 29. They had flown 22,000 miles (35,000 km). The remaining 7,000 miles (11,000 km) of the journey would be over the Pacific Ocean.

On July 2, 1937, Earhart and Noonan took off from Lae, heading for Howland Island 2,556 miles (4,113 km) away. The ship **USCGC** *Itasca* was stationed at Howland, ready to communicate with Earhart's Lockheed Electra and guide them to the island once they were nearby. As Earhart approached Howland Island, *Itasca* received radio messages from her. However, she could not hear the return messages from the ship. The ship's radio operator, Leo Bellarts, realized with horror that the aircraft's direction finder was not working—and there was nothing he could do about it.

Earhart radioed, "We must be on you, but cannot see you. Gas is running low. Have been unable to reach you by radio. We are flying at 1,000 feet (305 m)." They used the ship's boilers to create smoke to show their position, but it soon became clear that the fliers did not see it. The radio messages stopped.

A search for the missing aviators started within an hour after their last message was received and lasted until July 19. No trace of the plane or its occupants were found. In 1991, a piece of debris from Earhart's Electra was recovered from an uninhabited island. Is it possible Earhart landed near the island and become a castaway, eventually dying there?

The Sound Barrier

Chuck Yeager

During World War II, a number of pilots began to report undesirable aerodynamic effects as they approached the **speed of sound** in their aircraft. These effects were seen as a barrier, making **supersonic** speed very difficult, if not impossible, to achieve. Breaking the sound barrier became the next goal in the history of aviation.

After the war, the United States Air Force selected Charles "Chuck" Yeager to fly a rocket-powered aircraft to research high-speed flight. Chuck Yeager was a fighter pilot ace and a test pilot at Muroc Army Air Field (now Edwards Air Force Base). By October 14, 1947, the experimental rocket plane called Bell X-1 was finally ready for its flight to break the sound barrier.

Unknown to the authorities, however, two nights earlier Chuck Yeager had fallen off his horse and broken two ribs. He was so afraid of being taken off the mission that he went to a nearby veterinarian for treatment, and only told his wife and fellow project pilot Jack Ridley about the accident. On the day of the flight, Chuck was in so much pain that he could not even close Bell X-1's hatch. Luckily, Ridley came to his rescue and, using a chopped-down broom handle, rigged up a device to make it easier for Chuck to close the hatch.

The rocket plane was attached to the belly of a B-50 bomber which took off and released the X-1 at 30,000 feet (9,144 m). Chuck fired the rocket motors and the bullet-shaped plane accelerated to 807 mph (1,298.5 kph), or **Mach** 1.06, breaking the sound barrier.

On December 12, 1953, shortly after reaching Mach 2.44 (1,857 mph or 2,989 kph), Chuck lost control of a X-1A at 80,000 feet (24,000 m). In less than a minute, the plane fell 51,000 feet (16,000 m). It was only Chuck's extraordinary skills as a pilot that enabled him to bring the plane back under control and land safely.

Edwards Airforce Base — NORTH AMERICA

PACIFIC OCEAN

Stratospheric Skydive

Felix Baumgartner

Sixty-five years after Chuck Yeager broke the sound barrier in a rocket plane, daredevil skydiver Felix Baumgartner set out to become the first person to accomplish the same feat—but without a plane! The 43-year-old Austrian planned to jump from a specially-constructed balloon at over 128,000 feet (39 km) above Earth to break the world record for high-altitude skydives and speeds in **free fall**.

Years in the planning, Baumgartner and his team had gone through countless tests of equipment and practice jumps. Finally, on October 14, 2012, they were ready to make the record-breaking attempt from Roswell, New Mexico. Baumgartner used a specially-designed balloon with a pressurized capsule suspended beneath. He had to ascend to an altitude several times higher than the flight paths of commercial jets. He wore a highly reinforced space suit, which provided him with oxygen, as well as protected him from the -70°F (-56.7°C) temperature of the **stratosphere**.

When Baumgartner reached the required height, he depressurized the capsule. Then he launched himself out of the opened hatch. The thin atmosphere provided little resistance as he hurtled toward Earth, traveling at 730 mph (1,175 kph). Within a minute, he had broken the sound barrier! Suddenly, he lost control and went into a spin. Baumgartner was in danger of becoming unconscious and potentially a **redout**, leading to brain injury. Eventually he was able to regain control of his dive. As he fell, the

drag of the atmosphere began to slow him down. After four minutes and 22 seconds, he pulled his rip cord to activate his parachute. Baumgartner landed unharmed after traveling 24 miles (39 km) back to Earth.

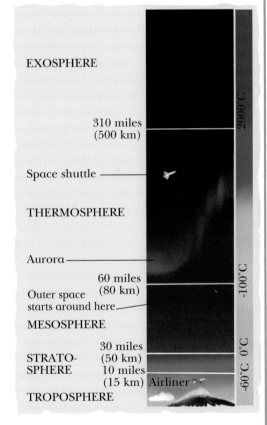

EXOSPHERE

310 miles
(500 km)

Space shuttle

THERMOSPHERE

Aurora

60 miles
(80 km)
Outer space
starts around here

MESOSPHERE

30 miles
(50 km)
STRATO-
SPHERE   10 miles
(15 km) Airliner

TROPOSPHERE

2000°C

-100°C

-60°C 0°C

Baumgartner set the world altitude record for skydiving at 24 miles (39 km), and was the first person to break the sound barrier in free fall. In 2014, American Alan Eustace jumped from over 130,000 feet (39.6 km) in a special space suit, and hit a top speed of 822 mph (1,323 kph) during a free fall.

Glossary

altitude A measurement of vertical distance

alum A chemical that resists flame

bog Wet, spongy ground

brigade A group of people organized for a purpose

ditch To make a forced landing on water

drag A force that slows forward motion

envelope A bag that holds gas for a balloon or airship

fixed-wing Describing wings that attach to an aircraft

free fall The part of a jump done without engaging a parachute

Mach A number that compares the speed of a body to the speed of sound

monoplane A fixed-wing aircraft with one main set of wings

navigation The science of getting a vehicle from place to place

radio compass A device that uses radio waves to find direction

speed of sound The distance traveled per unit of time by a sound wave

stratosphere Upper part of the atmosphere, 7 miles (11.25 km) or higher

supersonic Faster than the speed of sound

USCGC United States Coast Guard Cutter

Index